TRAFFIC SAFETY

Printed in the United States of America.

Library of Congress Cataloging-in-Publication Data
Loewen, Nancy, 1964
Traffic Safety/Nancy Loewen
p.   cm.
Summary: Offers rules for safe behavior on streets and sidewalks.
ISBN 1-56766-254-4
1. Traffic safety--United States--Juvenile literature.
2. Pedestrians--United States--Safety measures--Juvenile literature.
[1. Traffic safety.   2. Pedestrians.   3. Safety.]
I. Title.
HE5614.2.L63   1996
613.6'8--dc20   95-25897
                                        CIP
                                        AC

TRAFFIC SAFETY

By Nancy Loewen   Illustrated by Penny Dann

THE CHILD'S WORLD

Streets and sidewalks are all around us. They connect us to the places we want to go. But no matter where you go you need to observe some important rules. These rules will help prevent you or someone else from getting hurt. Pickles and Roy will show you what to do—and what not to do—to stay safe.

Never run into the street. Make it a habit to stop at the curb or edge of the road.

left right left

Before crossing the street, check for traffic by looking left, right, and left once more. Be sure to check for turning cars, too. If your view is blocked, edge out slowly and look again.

Use your ears as well as your eyes to check for traffic.
You might be able to hear cars that you can't yet see.

Obey traffic signals. Walk when the light is green, or when you see the walk signal. Even when you're crossing with the light, or at a stop sign, you still need to check for traffic in all directions.

Cross only at corners, and stay within the crosswalk if there is one. If you cross elsewhere, drivers won't be expecting you and they may not be able to stop in time. It's especially hard for drivers to see you if you run out from between parked cars.

Walk **briskly** as you cross the street. If you run, you could easily fall.

If you **dawdle**, more traffic could come along.

Try to avoid crossing the street at busy **intersections**. Ask your parents which streets in your neighborhood are safe to cross.

Walk on the sidewalk whenever possible. If there is no sidewalk, walk on the left side of the road, facing traffic. You'll be able to see oncoming cars, and the drivers will be able to see you better, too.

Don't play in the street or in parking lots. Go to a park, playground, or yard instead.

Watch out for cars backing out of driveways and parking spaces. Remember to watch for motorcycles and bicycles—they're vehicles, too.

If you see or hear emergency vehicles, move out of the way immediately. Don't let one accident turn into two!

Stay far away from snowplows, street-cleaning machines, garbage trucks, cement trucks and other vehicles that have special equipment. The drivers need to **concentrate** on their jobs and they may not see you.

If you have to be out after dark, be sure to stay on well-lit streets. If that's not possible, make yourself **visible** by wearing light-colored clothing and carrying a flashlight.

When you're a passenger in a vehicle, you need to follow some special rules, too. Always wear your seat belt, even on short trips. It' your best protection from getting hurt in an accident.

Wrong ↑

right ↙

The shoulder strap and the lap belt should both be snug.

Remind other passengers in the car to wear their seat belts, too. If passengers complain that it's not comfortable, tell the passengers that it will protect them from getting hurt in an accident.

Keep your head, arms, and feet inside the windows, and don't bother the driver.

Always check for traffic before opening the car door. In busy areas, get out of the car by the curb instead of on the street.

Never hitchhike . . .

. . . hang on to the back of a vehicle. . .

. . . or play near railroad tracks.

These are all very
dangerous things to do.

Follow these rules every time you're out and about, and remind your friends to follow them, too. That way you can all stay safe on the street!

Glossary

brisk (BRISK)
an energetic, quick, and alert pace. Walk briskly as you cross the street.

dawdle (DAH-dull)
to move slowly. If you dawdle while crossing the street, more traffic could come along.

intersection (IN-tur-sect-shon)
a place where two or more things meet. Try to avoid crossing at busy intersections.

concentrate (KON-sin-trate)
to turn ones attention to a specific thing. Drivers need to concentrate on the road.

visible (viz-e-bol)
capable of being seen. Carry a flashlight to make yourself visible at night.